ZONE 1
Leadership

Being a Fully Effective,
Selfless, and Genuine Leader

Dr. Michael P. Evans
Robert S. Walsh, MBA

Copyright © 2012 EACC Press: A division of EACC.
www.zone1leadership.com

All Rights Reserved
No part of this book may be reproduced, stored in a retrieval system, or transmitted by any means, electronic, mechanical, photocopying, recording, or other-wise, without the written permission from the publisher at www.zone1leadership.com.

Evans, Michael P. and Robert S. Walsh
    ZONE 1 Leadership: Being a Fully Effective, Selfless, and Genuine Leader

p.cm.

ISBN: 10: 0-9852420-2-7
ISBN-13: 978-0-9852420-2-2

1. Business. 2. Leadership. 3.Organizational Change.
Printed in the United States of America
10 9 8 7 6 5 4 3 2 1

All trademarks are the property of their respective companies.

About the Authors

Michael Evans and Robert Walsh have together provided leadership and organizational development consulting services for many years.

They are both veterans of the U.S. Navy, with Michael having served as an Expeditor in the Seabees for 6 years, and Robert as a Nuclear Propulsion Plant Supervisor for 23 years in the Submarine Service.

Their Naval service literally made them polar opposites, with Michael having served at Operation Deep Freeze in Antarctica, and Robert having operated under the ice at the North Pole.

They both hail from upstate New York, Michael from Oneida, and Robert from Syracuse. Robert relocated to the Detroit, MI metro area in 2004 where he currently resides.

Zone 1 Leadership is their first book written together.

The Symbol of Selfless Leadership

The box represents the team. The arrows within the box symbolize the leader serving the team. The arrows extending beyond the box symbolize the leader serving the organization. Selfless service by the leader is the common thread.

Contents

About the Authors iii

Prologue

    Why This Book Was Written 5

Chapter One

    Overview of ZONE Leadership 11
    The Concept of Leadership ZONES 14
    The Leadership ZONES 15
    Key Points of Chapter One 17

Chapter Two

    ZONE 1 Leaders 19
    Natural vs. Developed Leader 20
    Selfless Leadership 22
    Understanding ZONE 1 Leadership 23
    Leadership vs. Management Confusion 25
    Key Points of Chapter Two 27

Chapter Three

ZONE 2 Leaders 29
The "Self-Disabled" ZONE 2 Leader 31
The "Imposed Upon" ZONE 2 Leader 34
The "Out For #1" ZONE 2 Leader 36
Key Points of Chapter Three 38

Chapter Four

ZONE 3 Leaders 39
Key Points of Chapter Four 48

Chapter Five

ZONE 4 Leaders 49
Key Points of Chapter Five 53

Chapter Six

ZONE Leadership and the Culture Each Creates 55
Zone 1 Organizational Culture 56
    Evaluation and Accountability in ZONE 1 Organizations 59
    ZONE 1 Culture Summary 60
Zone 2 Organizational Culture 61
    Evaluation and Accountability in ZONE 2 Organizations 65
    ZONE 2 Culture Summary 66
Zone 3 Organizational Culture 67
Zone 4 Organizational Culture 70
Key Points of Chapter Six 71

Chapter Seven

How to Move to a ZONE 1 Culture 73
The ZONE 1 Leader Development Process 75
The ZONE 1 Organizational Culture 79
Development Process 79
The Role of Formal Assessment Tools 83
Key Points of Chapter Seven 85

Appendix A

How to Set Effective Development Goals 87

Appendix B

The Role Our Values Play In ZONE 1 Development 93

Appendix C

The Three Essential Skills of Open and Honest Communication 97
    Patient Listening 97
    How To Be A Properly Assertive Leader 99
    Concern for and Understanding The Real Needs Of Others 102

Appendix D

A Message for ZONE 2, 3, and 4 Leaders on Mentoring 105

Appendix E

A Collection of Key Points 109

Acknowledgements 115

Prologue

Why This Book Was Written

During our 25 years of leadership and organizational consulting, we have heard our clients ask many times, "What does it take to be a great leader and great organization?"

Everything we have ever seen that attempted to answer these questions, could not answer them.

The shelves in book stores and offices of senior executives are filled with books that offer advice, systems, and assessment instruments to identify an individual's character traits; such as understanding your 10-Killer Constraints (Flippen Profile©) or 34-Strengths (Clifton StrengthsFinder©). These tools do add value, but it is limited by how this heightened awareness is used.

Other books offer some version of "The list of things that make a great leader." But in reality, no list can ever be long enough because we are dealing with human beings and human behavior in dynamic situations.

In other words, the most important quality a leader needs at any given moment is different from the last, and unless we are able to consider these dynamics, the list will simply leave us thinking, "That wasn't on the list, what do I do now?"

The conventional wisdom for using these resources begins with an excellent goal– the organization wanting to further develop or provide continuing education to its leaders. A certain philosophy is typically chosen as "the way," which may be a book or an assessment instrument. The major difficulty with this approach is how the survey results or wisdom provided are used.

For instance, it's quite common for an organization to provide a feedback tool of some sort, tell leaders that the results are theirs alone to see, and task them to use this feedback to improve their leadership skills. Sometimes follow up coaching or training is provided, but most times the leaders are left to fare for themselves.

Essentially these leaders are given "snapshots' of feedback or wisdom as stand-alone tools, without follow up or continuity.

Some leaders will produce tangible benefits using this method, but many will not, preferring to suppress what they learned and stay in their comfort zones.

And in the final step of ineffectiveness, there is typically no accountability or reassessment to measure changes made or the results of those changes.

This also extends to the organizational level where climate survey results are frequently held too close to the chest of senior leaders, who may take some actions, but who usually don't share the results with many others. Or worse, they review the survey results and file them away on a shelf. Every organization would likely agree that this is inappropriate from a personnel and financial responsibility viewpoint.

These well intentioned efforts are ineffective because they miss the essential truth - that the culture is actually the product of the leadership.

To change the culture, one must start by changing how the leaders lead.

Realizing this we set out to describe what does count in the real world development of leaders and organizations, the concept of leadership ZONES developed.

Leadership ZONES describe our individual **awareness** and **how we use that awareness** to develop as leaders and create great organizational cultures.

The basis of using Leadership ZONES to develop leaders and organizations properly involves three significant systems:

❶ **Mentoring System.** A formal mentoring system promotes a dynamic level of information and a culture that develops and fosters personal growth with the focus on team outcome.

An effective mentoring system has leaders at every level of the organization, from the CEO to the line staff, participate in developing and maintaining themselves as fully effective leaders. The reality is that cultural change only occurs when all leaders are open about development and are actively involved in assisting each other in reaching their development goals.

The outcome of such change results in eliminating egos, politics, and other inefficient roadblocks, fostering the emergence of traits and behaviors of honesty and openness at all levels of the organization.

❷ **Accountability System.** Leaders must be properly and fairly evaluated on their leadership abilities and provided with ongoing feedback and awareness of the culture they are producing. Leaders must be held accountable for the results of their actions including the development of all subordinate leaders in their chain of command. Lack of this organizational accountability passively endorses ineffective leaders to remain in their comfort zone, resulting in a culture that does not promote and support the growth, direction, and outcome of the team.

Methods of accountability include the use of 360-degree assessments and organizational culture assessments (not simple climate surveys), coupled with performance reviews.

This ultimately eliminates the opportunity for "padded" performance reviews, which many individuals use to ensure their true performance (based on the reflection of their team) is hidden from what is actually occurring.

In a ZONE 1 Leadership system, evaluations are based on reality and measurable facts, and allow mechanisms to properly develop staff, their supervisors, and individuals above them. Proper evaluations ensure individuals become aware, develop strategies for growth, and implement developmental goals for success with the support of a mentor, except if they desire not to. In such cases, the organization will quickly realize this behavior and conscious choice, and act on removing them (not transferring them) from the ZONE 1 team for the betterment of the organization.

❸ **Integrated System.** Support from the highest levels is vital to promote a proper attitude toward developing every leader into their full potential. Top leaders must set the example so that no subordinate leader could choose otherwise, which happens so often without this element.

The final product of our analysis is this book, "ZONE 1 Leadership." With respect to the courage it takes to change oneself, we hope you find it answers the question, "What does it take to be a great leader and great organization?" for you and your organization.

Chapter One

Overview of ZONE Leadership

To begin our discussion of Leadership ZONES, please consider the following story. Ask yourself, "Do any of these individuals remind me of myself or others I've interacted with?"

> *It was Tuesday and time for our weekly senior staff meeting. Paul, another longtime leader and friend, walked with me to the conference room. We both used to look forward to these meetings, but that enthusiasm has faded since our new company President took over six months ago.*
>
> *The former company President, Ms. Hampton, was a strong purposeful leader whom everyone looked up to. When she was here we all worked hard and we sincerely felt like a team. She had high expectations, but also an involved and helpful nature. She knew what was going on*

and communications were open and meaningful. I could go on, but it's sufficient to say that Ms. Hampton was a solid leader, a view that I know was shared by all of us.

Our new President, Mr. Astor is a nice enough person, but not focused it seems. When he first arrived he made it clear that he knew we were an accomplished team, and that his style was predominately Laissez-Faire. He declared his hands-off approach would work well as we were a proven team and could all obviously operate best with very with little direction from the top. It sounded like a fair assessment and a good way to go... at first. Now, six months later, well, I don't know.

Our staff meetings now seem to last forever and little real work gets accomplished or decisions made. We waste a lot of time now dealing with micro-details while the big picture slips away, and that seems to be the order of the day – unaware.

We seem to have lost our way, as everyone has reverted to their own comfort zones. Loyalty to the team has steadily decreased, and the behavior of the senior staff is very confusing. Paul and I have talked about it many times. We agreed that now, instead of a good team, the senior staff had devolved into factions based on power, or so it appears.

Some leaders seem to want to control everything, like Robert Smith. It feels like he could care less how others are affected, and this from a man I would have called an involved team-player in the past.

Others on the senior staff have gone in the opposite direction and just given up it seems, deferring to "whatever."

And in one very surprising instance, I observed a senior staff member, John Noble, literally promise the world to the President, then complain to subordinates and do nothing!

Most depressing in all of this is that Mr. Astor seems to be clueless about what is happening, even after Paul and I went to see him. He just gave us some "mumbo-jumbo" about staff now being free to make the best choices rather than being confined by his involvement, and that others had told him they liked having the leash slackened.

My frustration is very high, and I've had more than one discussion with Paul about moving on to a company that is smart about whom they put in charge. But, well - I guess I'm just "venting" because I could never leave and throw my team to the dogs. I've been successful at filtering this stuff and keeping my subordinate leaders and their teams on track, but it's well known that things are going downhill with the senior staff. This is starting to permeate throughout the company with great speed and negativity. Loyalty and respect are slipping away fast. I wish there were something more Paul and I could do.

The Concept of Leadership ZONES

We've all experienced people in positions of power who seem to have trouble understanding and using that power effectively. As in the story above, they appear to have settled into a personal zone of comfort which overrides their basic common sense and responsibility to those they lead.

This is similar to something I experienced during my MBTI© (Myers-Briggs Type Indicator) certification training. After four days of observing our instructor, he asked us if we thought him to be an introvert or an extrovert. Well it was obvious - He was an excellent instructor; engaging, dynamic, and energized by what he was doing. Clearly he was an extrovert, so we were quite surprised when he disclosed himself to be an introvert!

In discussing this, the class concurred that being an instructor is an extrovert-oriented skill. Significantly, the sharing of energy in a very external way is required to be an effective instructor, and this does not come naturally to an introvert. His natural tendency is toward inward energy.

Our instructor had developed these extrovert-natural instructor skills because he was aware that it was necessary to consciously achieve a different comfort zone to be effective as an instructor. He had worked hard and had genuinely developed that comfort zone, so that to the outside observer, it looked natural.

However, because he is an introvert at heart – a fact that cannot be changed – his true natural comfort zone will always be inward and if he were not consciously aware of this, he might retreat to his natural comfort zone at the wrong time. Now, this is unlikely when he's consciously in "instructor mode," but with Leadership ZONE behavior, the natural and unconscious tendency to go to your comfort zone and avoid your discomfort zones is much more pervasive and subtle.

The Leadership ZONES

There are four ZONES which we will discuss in detail throughout the following chapters. The following will give an overview of the basic tenets of where individuals are in respect to being leaders.

ZONE 1	ZONE 2	ZONE 3	ZONE 4
Fully Developed, Fully Conscious	*Not Fully Developed, Fully Conscious*	*Not Fully Developed, Somewhat Conscious*	*Not Developed, Not Conscious*
ZONE 1 – Fully Effective Selfless Genuine Leader	ZONE 2 – Aware of Weaknesses and that Development is Needed	ZONE 3 – Limited Awareness of Actual Weaknesses or Need For Development	ZONE 4 – Unaware of Weaknesses or Need For Development

ZONE 1: The ZONE 1 Leader may have natural or developed leadership skills and is operating in a highly effective zone of comfort. They are not perfect, but are aware of the impact of their actions. Their basic paradigm is selfless and they are open to changing as necessary to ensure their actions are in the best interest of the team and the organization.

ZONE 2: The ZONE 2 Leader is aware of their shortfalls and is aware of the impact of their actions. Some of these leaders are open to changing and are actively working to develop into ZONE 1 Leaders. If they are not open to change, they are intentionally limiting their leadership effectiveness.

ZONE 3: The ZONE 3 Leader has a limited awareness of their shortfalls and is only somewhat aware of the full impact of their actions. Their ability to change is a "shot in the dark" because they do not have a clear understanding of what or how to change.

ZONE 4: The ZONE 4 Leader tends to have advanced to their position based on technical skills or seniority and therefore has a strong belief in their own competence. This illusionary self-confidence carries over to their leadership abilities as they are functionally unaware of their shortfalls. They believe they are effective leaders and as a result have little motivation to further develop.

Clearly, the development of highly effective leadership skills by the person entrusted to lead a team is foundational to the team they lead. As leaders, we owe it to those we lead to be the best leaders we can be. When we come up against our limitations and zones of discomfort while providing that leadership, if we retreat back to where we feel personally comfortable, we may be selling ourselves, our team, or the organization short.

In the following chapters we will investigate each of these ZONEs in detail, including clear-cut actions to move toward being a ZONE 1 Leader.

Key Points of Chapter One

1. Leadership skills are different from other job skills and must be acknowledged as a unique skill-set.

2. Leaders may settle into zones of comfort, or zones that avoid discomfort. While either of these may seem personally correct, they can be destructive if they are not also right for the team.

3. ZONE 1 Leaders are fully effective selfless genuine leaders. ZONE 1 Leadership skills can be developed as we come across our limitations and use them to our advantage.

Chapter Two

ZONE 1 Leaders

ZONE 1	ZONE 2	ZONE 3	ZONE 4
Fully Developed, Fully Conscious	*Not Fully Developed, Fully Conscious*	*Not Fully Developed, Somewhat Conscious*	*Not Developed, Not Conscious*
ZONE 1 – Fully Effective Selfless Genuine Leader	ZONE 2 – Aware of Weaknesses and that Development is Needed	ZONE 3 – Limited Awareness of Actual Weaknesses or Need For Development	ZONE 4 – Unaware of Weaknesses or Need For Development

We previously stated that the ZONE 1 Leader may have natural or developed leadership skills and is operating in a highly effective zone of comfort. ZONE 1 Leaders are not perfect, but are aware of the impact of their actions. They are selfless and open to changing as necessary to ensure their actions are in the best interest of the team and the organization.

As you and I work with ZONE 1 Leaders, we may come to think of them as "natural leaders," instead of those who developed their leadership traits with intention. Let's take a look at this notion and the differences between the natural and the developed leader.

Natural vs. Developed Leader

From early childhood and throughout their formative years, the natural leader has had their leadership traits engrained in them. Their parents and other influential individuals mentored them with openness and honesty, so that the values and traits they possess seem quite natural and even intrinsic to them.

So-called "natural leaders" are guided by a selfless value system that supports understanding the personal and interpersonal aspects of their actions as they relate to the greater service of others. They are perceived as being totally honest and trustworthy.

They seem to naturally think in terms of what is right for the team they are a part of, as this is their personal preference. They lead from any position they find themselves in, never limited by title, pay grade, or official rules.

Decision making and effectively communicating the course of action they decide upon is so clear to the natural leader that everyone tends to quickly get behind it, and at times, tend to mirror and aspire to act in the same decisive way.

However, the natural leader is not perfect. They engage in constant self-assessment and feedback to ensure maximum effectiveness and growth in order to hone their skills. In other words, there actually is a developmental aspect essential to the so-called "natural leader."

The developed leader, on the other hand, consciously decides to develop their leadership values and traits. This does not come naturally and is frequently sparked by a need growing out of a significant event or events in their lives. In other words, when the errors they make become significant enough the need to develop becomes obvious to them they push themselves to take action.

Lacking the elemental framework that the natural leader possesses, the developed leader must work consciously so that they start to think as the natural leader does. This journey is not an easy one for most. It is a constant push and pull of emotions, habits and ideas which plague one to revert to what they did before.

When the developed leader has achieved their goal of thinking and behaving like the natural leader, the differences between them become indistinguishable to others. They are both equally effective which is why developed leaders may look like natural leaders to others.

*Their different paths to success are immaterial –
Both natural and developed ZONE 1 Leaders
are Fully Effective
Selfless Genuine Leaders.*

Selfless Leadership

In leadership as in all other things, we excel at certain aspects and have weaknesses in other areas. It is likely that we feel very comfortable and confident in doing what we excel at, and likewise less confident, uncomfortable, and unsure when doing what we feel weaker at. These zones of comfort and discomfort exist in every leader. How we deal with them defines us as leaders.

As leaders, choosing to lead from our comfort zones is fundamentally selfish. Zone 1 Leaders do not allow themselves to do this. Instead, they understand that the very cornerstone of honorable leadership is to serve those we lead, and overcome our weaknesses and flaws to do so.

The difference that makes selfless leaders effective is that when faced with taking action that is personally uncomfortable, they push through their discomfort and do what is right rather than choosing self first.

Selfless service is the hallmark of being a genuine leader. To do anything less is simply not acceptable.

Understanding ZONE 1 Leadership

So, what is a ZONE 1 Leader? What makes a leader fully effective, selfless, and genuine? Consider the following:

> *My name is Susan Rodgers. I lead the project management group for our company's operations in the mid-west. We recently received a highly visible and politically sensitive project. My group was tasked with coordinating all efforts of the company nationwide, as well as sub-contractors and government oversight elements. This was a great opportunity for us and the company, and our reputation and future opportunities for the firm were definitely on the line. As they say, with great opportunity comes great risk. Accordingly, I took the time to really think this out before I briefed my team.*
>
> *On Monday I gathered them together. I began to draw an outline of how I saw the project unfolding, and after a couple of minutes, Bill Carnegie, one of my senior planners raised his hand. "Boss, we've been through a lot of projects and I think we really know what we're doing. How about if you leave and let the rest of us plan this one out. We'll come and get you when we're ready to present it to you."*
>
> *I stopped and said, "Give me a minute."*
>
>> *I thought to myself... Well the team is very senior and they do have decades of technical experience, that is except for Andrea and Kelly, but the senior folks could make sure they are included. On the other hand, this might be risky. All the home office*

executives will be watching this one VERY closely, but then the team knows that. Can I trust them? Yes, of course, and after all, they are asking me for this, what more could I want as a leader? Besides, I will have the final say and we have time. Why not?

"Okay, that sounds good," I said. Just to be clear, we need the final plan done by this Friday, so I'll need to go over it with you a day or two ahead of time. Does Wednesday at 1:00 P.M. work for everyone's schedule?" The team all agreed except Allen who had a conflicting deadline, but he said he'd adjust it as this project took precedence.

"One more thing," I said. "Andrea and Kelly are still in training and I want to make sure they learn all they can from this, so for you senior folks, please be sure that happens." Bill Carnegie said, "Consider it done - any other questions or concerns boss?"

"No, you've got the football, have fun!" I left the room confident that things would go well.

What happened during this meeting may seem a little benign at first glance. That tends to be the nature of ZONE 1 Leadership - on target with everything fitting well. Clearly Susan was indeed fully effective and genuine with her team being the same. The team is indeed a reflection of her leadership.

Another way to look at this is by thinking about what could have happened if Susan were not a ZONE 1 Leader. There are a thousand ways she could have blown it. She could have been overly concerned with her own reputation and insisted on micromanaging things. She could have set deadlines without asking what worked or allowing any flexibility. We can all probably think of other ways we've seen leaders fail.

In that regard, ZONE 1 Leaders stand apart in that they consciously develop themselves toward making fewer and fewer mistakes. They strive to make each mistake only once, correct it, and then grow from it.

So the answer to our question, "What is a ZONE 1 Leader?" is somewhat ethereal in that there is no list of right and wrong to go by. Rather, ZONE 1 Leaders have the ability and flexibility to read and react to what is right for the team as things develop. They are not stuck in any pre-conceived box, rather, their box changes as the shape of things change. But, they always have things in the box, not out of control.

Leadership vs. Management Confusion

It is quite common to find people in supervisory positions who are excellent managers of policy, process, and procedure. They have highly developed skills in these areas. For many, these skills make up a comfort zone. After all, it's pretty natural to feel good about such things. But this is not leadership.

Leadership involves people. When we put people into the mix of policy, process, and procedure, a different skill set is necessary to properly influence them. Influencing others is the end game of leadership, and thus requires this entirely different skill set than management.

You can be a great manager but a poor leader. We've all seen this in action. But can you be a fully effective leader and also be a poor manager?

Some might see leadership and management skills as mutually exclusive, but a leader who lacks management skills is not fully efficient and therefore not fully effective – and not a ZONE 1 leader.

In order to be a fully effective ZONE 1 Leader, you must also be a fully effective manager.

Our Path From Here: The Other ZONES

Moving forward, we'll look at the other three ZONES, and compare and contrast them with ZONE 1, with details about how to develop from wherever you are into ZONE 1 Leadership.

Key Points of Chapter Two

1. Both natural and developed leaders operate in ZONE 1 as Fully Effective Selfless Genuine Leaders.

2. ZONE 1 Leaders make fewer and fewer mistakes as they continually develop. They strive to make each mistake only once, correct it, and then grow from it.

3. ZONE 1 Leaders have the ability to read and react to what is right for the team as things develop. They are not stuck in any pre-conceived box.

4. In order to be a fully effective ZONE 1 Leader, you must also be a fully effective manager.

5. Selfless service is the hallmark of being a genuine leader. To do anything less is simply not acceptable.

Chapter Three

ZONE 2 Leaders

ZONE 1	ZONE 2	ZONE 3	ZONE 4
Fully Developed, Fully Conscious	*Not Fully Developed, Fully Conscious*	*Not Fully Developed, Somewhat Conscious*	*Not Developed, Not Conscious*
ZONE 1 – Fully Effective Selfless Genuine Leader	ZONE 2 – Aware of Weaknesses and that Development is Needed	ZONE 3 – Limited Awareness of Actual Weaknesses or Need For Development	ZONE 4 – Unaware of Weaknesses or Need For Development

The primary advantage of being a ZONE 2 Leader is that you have an accurate awareness of your weaknesses and shortfalls and recognize that development is needed. How you deal with this knowledge though, tells the tale of whether you can use this awareness to develop toward ZONE 1 Leadership or not.

Some ZONE 2 Leaders are simply *"Moving through ZONE 2."* They are fully acting as a ZONE 1 Leader in that they know what their shortfalls are and are working effectively to correct them. They actively seek feedback, consistently do self-assessment, and work effectively with a mentor in addressing opportunities for growth. They are not in ZONE 1 yet, but only for lack of experience.

Next are the *"Self-Disabled"* ZONE 2 Leaders. They are stuck in behaviors that feel comfortable for them, though this may be wrong for their team and the organization as a whole. They may be very effective in some, or even many situations, but highly ineffective in others as a result of their personal needs overriding what they know to be proper leadership behavior. Most perplexing is that some of these leaders are comfortable in their inability because they are not held accountable; they have no fear of ramifications. The Self-disabled can recover from this with structure, accountability, and mentoring to become ZONE 1 leaders.

There are a small number of *"Imposed Upon"* ZONE 2 Leaders; those who've tried to change but have come up against actual inabilities within themselves. Certain necessary leadership functions are exceptionally difficult for them to perform. This is not by choice, rather they do not have these functions in them nor can they be developed. They should not have been advanced to leadership in the first place, and should be allowed to return to another job where they can be effective. The demands of leadership will take a human toll on such a person. Unfortunately, many organizations will not allow voluntary demotion, only having an "up or out" policy.

Last, a small group of ZONE 2 Leaders that we'll call *"Out for #1"* leaders know the right answers and fake proper leadership behavior, while actually staying in their zone of comfort. They look like fully effective leaders but this is only a front they put on for higher-ups. Therefore, higher-ups incorrectly see them as ZONE 1 Leaders. Their team knows the real person they are and knows they are out for themselves first.

The "Out for #1" leader can recover from this, but may only be able to change if a ZONE 1 higher-up takes the time to confront the truth with them, using documented accountability, developmental plans, mentoring and supervisory involvement. They can become ZONE 1 Leaders but they have the toughest hill to climb – confronting their true self with courage to change who they essentially are.

With the exception of the "Moving through ZONE 2" leaders, who require no further detailing here, we'll look at each of the other three manifestations of ZONE 2 Leadership a little closer.

The "Self-Disabled" ZONE 2 Leader

We have all experienced supervisors who know the right answers, but sometimes do the wrong things. This is puzzling because during those times, it is very obvious that these "Self-disabled" leaders are more concerned with their personal comfort or security over what they know to be proper leadership action. But for them, knowing and doing are two distinctly different things, with their needs usually winning out.

This need for personal comfort and security generally manifests itself in two ways. "Self-disabled" leaders either take action they know is wrong, or through fear, avoid acting when they know they should.

For instance, a leader may be disorganized and habitually late, wasting everyone's time. They are somehow content in their tardiness, and rather than change, they may laugh this off and tell others something like, "You know how I am!"

Typical for many "Self-disabled" leaders, the areas in which they demonstrate their misplaced motivations are very specific, yet they can be highly effective otherwise. For example, consider Jack – a team leader of four surveyors marking out a new flood control channel in the New Orleans area:

> *I (Jack) was so excited when I was put in charge of this team. We would be operating for months out in the back country on a very important and politically sensitive new project. Throughout the preliminary planning stages I was happier than I'd been in years; finally being able to get back to the field work I loved. You see, I was "promoted" five years ago to what essentially amounted to working on my own in a cube in the corner doing Quality Assurance. Now I was going to lead a team again and get muddy!*

Then I found out who was on my team and my heart sank. Jill Smith, or "Ornery Jill" as I like to think about her. She shows me no respect and refuses to do what I ask of her. A week ago I timidly tried to tell her to do something, and she got angry and meanly grunted, "Make me!" in front of the rest of the team. Now I barely see her and I really don't know what she's up to. Frankly I'm happy to have it that way – except – well, I am supposed to be in charge and responsible for what we accomplish. But what can I do? I'm just no good at confrontation. Hopefully Jill is doing something productive, but if not, I'm sure the rest of us will be able to fill in the gaps. At least the rest of the team works!

Jack is an effective manager with those who only need to be managed. But for those who need a leader, like Jill and those on the team that she is a part of, Jack is ineffective because he is more concerned with his own comfort than leading them.

Instead of dealing with Jill's insubordination, which is the right thing for his team, he allowed her to walk all over him. The rest of the team suffers for his inaction. Jill is also not doing well

> Emotions are natural and normal, and emotions being emotions, we'd all like to think that we are in ZONE 1 a majority of the time and that we shift to one of the other zones on occasion. But, putting our emotions aside for a minute, realize that ZONE 1 is an absolute – you are either there, or you are not. The ZONE 1 leader is the "Fully Effective Selfless Genuine Leader," and does not shift into another zone.

under his "Self-disabling" behavior. Her performance and job satisfaction are also part of Jack's responsibility, but the team and Jill are far from Jack's mind.

Sometimes a "Self-disabled" leader like Jack will talk openly about their shortfalls and their inability to change. As they describe it, they are somehow being victimized by their strong comfort and security needs. They feel quite powerless over them and lean on these to justify their behavior.

The "Imposed Upon" ZONE 2 Leader

Leaders who are "Imposed Upon" do have an accurate awareness of their weaknesses and recognizing the need to change. They have likely spent many futile hours seeking help and advice to try to find the right answer or technique that will resolve their inability to effectively do what they know they should. This is very frustrating as they try very hard, but just can't make things work for them. Consider the following:

> *My name is Walt and I hate my job. I would do anything to go back to my old desk. I've tried everything, but I just can't seem to get it right when it comes to getting others to work for me. They don't do what I tell them, and I end up having to step in and do things myself just to meet deadlines. It's very obvious to me that they don't respect me.*

I always thought that it would be great to be a supervisor. My father retired from the Air Force and is still to this day a recognized leader. My sister Alice is a lawyer for a multi-national corporation and leads a team of other lawyers working on environmental compliance. But unlike them, I just don't seem to have inherited the leadership gene.

I do have a mentor who I've been working with for the last six months. My boss also goes out of her way to try to help me. I've tried everything they suggested to no end.

Things are always fairly cordial; after all I used to be just another worker here before I was advanced. But when I try to shift and be the leader, I immediately feel the discomfort. I feel like a mouse, totally gun shy. My mentor and boss have both told me that I need to be firmer and more direct; that I sound too suggestive rather than giving clear direction. But every time I try, it comes out wrong.

It's eating my heart out. Confidentially I've stopped trying and just do the work myself to avoid beating myself up in front of my co-workers, I mean team members. I'm getting here earlier than ever and staying late, and my wife is pushing me hard to stop doing that. I feel like I'm aging faster and I just want to quit, but I still have 12 years to go until retirement.

I have asked to be allowed to go back to my old job, but my boss immediately told me that wasn't an option, and that I just needed to stick with it until I get it right. Nobody hears me, I swear. Oh, why did I ever take this job!

Does this sound like anyone you know or have ever known? Think of how much energy is being wasted trying to put Walt's square peg into a round hole.

The same people who advanced Walt without ensuring that he would have the skills and abilities he needs to lead are now telling him the decision is final. Clearly they are also ZONE 2 leaders that are likely "Self-disabled." They either knew, or at least now know, what is wrong with Walt, but are unwilling to effectively lead in this situation by doing what is right for both Walt and the team he leads.

Think about that for a minute. Clearly Walt is not an effective leader and this is not good for those he is in charge of, but the mentor and his boss just keep trying to fix Walt while the team continues to go downhill.

> *Every time you see a failing leader that is not being helped effectively, you are actually seeing at least two failing leaders, because it is the higher-up leader's responsibility to make sure their subordinate leaders are effective.*

The "Out For #1" ZONE 2 Leader

A while back, a leader at a company we were working with walked up to me in the hall and told me that she was being promoted to a national leadership position. I congratulated her heartily as she told me the details and how hard she'd worked to get the promotion. It was impressive to say the least.

A few moments later, I came across two of her subordinate leaders that I'd worked with in the past. I mentioned that she'd told me about her promotion and how impressive her efforts sounded to me. They both looked at each other and rolled their eyes. Then one of them grabbed my upper arm, pulled me close and whispered something like, "Just between us, she got that promotion by stepping all over the rest of us. She always makes sure she looks good and has hung us out to dry so many times that we've lost count. She's horrible, and let me tell you, we are all very happy she's leaving."

What a tragedy. This is not the right leader for a national position as her impact was now going to be much broader and affect far more people.

The leaders who selected her failed to do their job and have now advanced someone they shouldn't have. The irony is that there were many others below her level who knew the truth. It is also quite likely her peers and immediate supervisor knew the truth about her. So why didn't this information make it to the right ears?

There are many reasons that the truth about poor leadership performance doesn't come to light with higher-ups, but one particular factor is almost always at play; the higher-ups created a culture which favored keeping such things a secret and in the end, didn't ask the right people in the right way. Now she has been advanced to an even higher level of incompetence.

Again, every time you see a failing leader that is not being helped effectively, you are actually seeing at least two failing leaders, because it is the higher-up leader's responsibility to make sure their subordinate leaders are effective.

Key Points of Chapter Three

1. ZONE 2 leaders are fully conscious and aware of their weaknesses which can be a significant advantage if they use this awareness effectively.

2. ZONE 2 leaders may want to see themselves as being ZONE 1 except for having some shortfalls. This is not valid because part time effectiveness is simply not the same as being a "Fully Effective Selfless Genuine Leader"

3. Every time you see a failing leader that is not being helped effectively, you are actually seeing at least two failing leaders, because it is the higher-up leader's responsibility to make sure their subordinate leaders are effective.

Chapter Four

ZONE 3 Leaders

ZONE 1	ZONE 2	ZONE 3	ZONE 4
Fully Developed, Fully Conscious	*Not Fully Developed, Fully Conscious*	*Not Fully Developed, Somewhat Conscious*	*Not Developed, Not Conscious*
ZONE 1 – Fully Effective Selfless Genuine Leader	ZONE 2 – Aware of Weaknesses and that Development is Needed	ZONE 3 – Limited Awareness of Actual Weaknesses or Need For Development	ZONE 4 – Unaware of Weaknesses or Need For Development

ZONE 3 Leaders have a limited awareness of their shortfalls and are only somewhat aware of the full impact of their actions. Their ability to change is a "shot in the dark" because they do not have an accurate understanding of what or how to change.

Frequently a ZONE 3 Leader will have learned a tactic from other leaders and will attempt to simply follow what they have learned. However, because they lack a deep understanding of why this works, they are unable to generalize what they know or adapt it in a consistent way as events require.

Occasionally a ZONE 3 Leader can "Copycat" others effectively enough to look like a more developed leader, but because they have no real understanding, they are lost when there is no effective model to follow. "Copycat" activity is usually reactionary "tunnel-vision." It is a way of dealing with limited awareness. The hope is self-preservation.

ZONE 3 "tunnel-vision" may also be a result of an intentional act by the leader, an intentional denial of information by others, or an actual limitation of the individual's abilities.

The Interim Leader

A frequently seen example of intentional ZONE 3 tunnel-vision is with the interim leader. When a leadership position is left unfilled for some time, or "gapped" as it is sometimes called, it is commonplace to find someone to take on this position in an "interim" status, sometimes as a collateral duty.

Who is chosen is critical to the team. If the interim is a ZONE 1 leader, they will act in an effective manner until the new permanent leader arrives, which is of course what the team and the organization desire.

However, if the interim is a ZONE 2 "Self-disabled" or "Imposed upon" leader, or if they happen to be in ZONE 3, they could easily treat this assignment in the wrong way, such as seeing this assignment as a bother, or more likely, approaching it with fear.

Or, if the interim is a ZONE 2 "out-for-#1" leader, they may either see this as hindering their image with higher-ups, or as an opportunity to leverage it for their own benefit.

In any case, none of the attitudes that these ZONE 2 or ZONE 3 leaders bring to this assignment are desirable for the team. The evidence of this is what you and I have clearly heard from interims on many occasions, such things as, "I'm only here for emergencies," or "I'm only the interim and I'm not going to change anything or make any decisions unless I have to."

Or the clearly ZONE 3 speech, "I don't have much time, so I'll be at my regular desk and I'll check in from time-to-time. Don't get a hold of me unless it's really important. I'm sure you (the team) can handle all the routine stuff."

These types of statements guarantee that the interim will be operating as a ZONE 3 Leader in relation to filling this temporary position because they have created a "tunnel vision" environment for themselves. Interestingly, many around them (except for ZONE 1 Leaders), especially higher-ups, will treat their ignorance with an understanding attitude; after all, they are only there on a temporary basis.

One thing this commonly produces for the team is created crises. The ZONE 3 interim makes them jump through hoops to make up for his or her lack of awareness, especially when higher-ups push the interim for information or action from the team.

This underscores the main problem – what about the team? If the team was included as a primary consideration, then those choosing the interim leader would only have one choice – install a ZONE 1 Leader or a "Moving through ZONE 2" Leader as a developmental assignment coupled with a ZONE 1 mentor.

The Classic ZONE 3 Leader

As we previously observed, the main issue with being a ZONE 3 Leader stems from a limited awareness. In many real world instances, this results in the leader taking ineffective or inappropriate action. This undermines the ZONE 3 Leader's ability to lead as the team comes to see them as inept. This is not an unrecoverable position, and the ZONE 3 Leader can develop toward ZONE 1 Leadership, but only with the help of a solid ZONE 1 mentor who can open their eyes. Here is a true situation from the past of one of the authors, Robert Walsh, to illustrate this:

> *In 1985, I was a Chief Petty Officer in the U.S. Navy serving as a Nuclear Propulsion Plant Supervisor onboard the fast attack submarine, U.S.S. Parche (SSN-683). I had twenty-three nuclear trained personnel working for me. These men*

were literally the cream of the crop. Navy "nukes" as they are called, are among the smartest and most capable people in the nation, easily in the top 10% of the Navy.

Down the hall, or passageway, from the crew's mess, or enlisted dining facility, was the "Leader-board" that had about two dozen brass nameplates mounted on it. Each was engraved with the name of one of the management staff that currently held leadership positions onboard the ship. Some of these nameplates were shiny and new, some were older and tarnished, and all were in their proper place… except mine.

One fateful day, mine went missing.

I found out it was gone when I went to go to the restroom, or head as it's called, back in the engine room. I looked down, and there, glued to the back wall of the urinal, was my nameplate!

I blew a gasket! Everyone who worked for me probably had a truly delightful time urinating on my nameplate and laughing their butts off! I threw open the door with anger for all to see. We have a saying in the Submarine Force for times like these:

> **When in trouble, or in doubt,**
> **run in circles, scream and shout**

This was wisdom lost on the forlorn nameplate owner. I grabbed the first poor soul I could find and "supervised" as he removed the nameplate and gave it to me - after he had sanitized it.

I went off into a corner, nameplate in hand, to stew. Alone now, the reality of it all hit me in the chest – full force.

Oh my God! My own people, the ones I was in charge of, hated working for me. Worse, to do this, they must actually hate me as a person. This was feedback of the worst kind and it ate at my heart. Raw, accurate, and intensely hurtful feedback.

How the hell did this happen to me? I was devastated. I was a rotten leader. They knew it and I knew it too.

I was also very fortunate because one of the greatest leaders who ever walked the earth was there to help turn this into the pivotal moment in my life as a leader. His name is Howard Swain, and he was the Chief-of-the-Boat, or "COB."

Howard always seemed to know everything that went on. He walked up, put his hand on my shoulder and said something like, "Bob, I heard about the nameplate, and I'm going to tell you the truth... You don't know what the hell you're doing!"

How true. How painfully true. Howard never pulled a punch.

He went on, "When you're ready, which needs to be right now, we'll talk and help you fix this problem."

Howard became my mentor.

I didn't know it at the time, but over the course of the next eighteen months, Howard would teach me applied leadership like no other could. He was always there with his patient ear and easy-going style to help, guide, coach, and most importantly – to model excellence in leadership for me. Chiefly he'd ask me questions and help me figure out the angles as each small challenge or situation arose. Sometimes he'd give me the right words to say. Sometimes he'd just stand back and tell me to figure it out for myself.

I came to understand how I got in these shoes. I knew I had been a good leader until I got advanced to Chief Petty Officer. But then I made a fatal error, or series of them to be accurate.

To start with, I had tried to be the same guy I was before I put that uniform on. I had been an easy going, very friendly leader of a different group on another ship. They were peers and subordinates, and they were also my buddies and friends. I wanted that to be the same as a Chief, but I didn't understand that my new team wouldn't see me in the same way because I was now a Chief.

So, I was either coming across as their buddy or pal, or when that failed – another great mistake– I got very coercive with predictable results. My people distanced themselves from me because they didn't know who was going to show up that day. Maybe it would be nice Chief Walsh whose inappropriate over-friendliness made them feel uncomfortable, or nasty Chief Walsh who jammed things down their throats. I happily distanced myself from them as well, and all of this got me in trouble.

I became almost completely ignorant of what was going on with my men. I had no clue about what was happening in their lives outside of work, or on the job. It became commonplace for me to show up and be the last to know, when I was expected to be a real Chief and be the pivotal person. Anyway, things degraded further and I hated being there.

I'm sure you could see it in my eyes; I certainly could when I looked in the mirror or in the eyes of those I led. I had little or no confidence. I frequently could feel a certain hollowness in my chest. I had trouble sleeping and relations with my family became strained. I hated going to work and actually tried to hide during the day. I looked forward to vacations, holidays, and sick days as brief moments of "relief."

But all this changed with Howard as my mentor.

Over the next year and a half, my confidence grew and Howard's presence shifted from mentor to colleague. What a great feeling to possess the confidence that comes from real world experience, for which there is no substitute. I owe a great deal to Howard Swain's guidance and patience. Thank you Howard!

Howard was clearly a ZONE 1 leader and because of this, was able to assess and take action to help move this ZONE 3 leader into ZONE 1. This evidenced itself even before the incident with his waiting for the right time and set of circumstances so that the ZONE 3 leader would be ready to change. Then *"He was always there with his patient ear and easy-going style to help, guide, coach, and most importantly to model excellence in leadership."*

Clearly there are many things we can learn from this situation, not the least of which being that nearly everyone can develop themselves into a ZONE 1 leader, with proper assistance. This is true even for leaders who have serious weaknesses and shortfalls.

But to get to ZONE 1, the developing leader needs a mentor who is already there, and a mentor who is not in ZONE 1 is not going to be fully effective in this regard.

Key Points of Chapter Four

1. Care needs to be taken when choosing who to put in charge, whether in an interim situation or as part of the regular selection process.

2. Leaders who are ineffective can develop themselves into ZONE 1, with proper assistance.

3. ZONE 1 Leaders are able to be fully effective mentors. Mentors who are not in ZONE 1 themselves will not be fully effective mentors.

Chapter Five

ZONE 4 Leaders

ZONE 1	ZONE 2	ZONE 3	ZONE 4
Fully Developed, Fully Conscious	*Not Fully Developed, Fully Conscious*	*Not Fully Developed, Somewhat Conscious*	*Not Developed, Not Conscious*
ZONE 1 – Fully Effective Selfless Genuine Leader	ZONE 2 – Aware of Weaknesses and that Development is Needed	ZONE 3 – Limited Awareness of Actual Weaknesses or Need For Development	ZONE 4 – Unaware of Weaknesses or Need For Development

ZONE 4 Leaders tend to have advanced to their position based on technical skills or seniority and therefore have a strong belief in their own competence. This illusionary self-confidence carries over to their leadership abilities as they are functionally unaware of their shortfalls. They believe they are effective leaders and as a result have little motivation to further develop.

This belief can be so strong that it limits their ability to receive feedback about their performance. They may look with puzzlement at another who is trying to tell them about their performance, shrug them off, and return to their comfort zone. They think that the other individual is the one who doesn't get it. They believe their actions to be those of highly effective leaders and see their actions as doing what is best for the team; after all, they know best and are right in their own perception.

This type of leader is likely to have the most difficulty understanding their shortcomings and resist making the transition to move toward ZONE 1. They will likely require a very strong, mature, and senior ZONE 1 Leader to be their mentor as this process of change for the ZONE 4 will probably involve numerous repetitive reinforcements. Please consider the following:

> *Bryce Phillips was a student in a year-long senior leadership development program we conducted. Bryce was certainly a "wise acre." For instance; he claims that he was actually born on the electrical maintenance shop floor. He started there 32 years ago right out of school and this is the only company he has ever worked for. He started out sweeping the floor and learned what he could here and there from the electricians doing maintenance. He eventually worked himself up to a point where the company sent him to trade school, and after 20 years of hard work, he became the head of electrical repair and maintenance.*

I remember the first time he spoke in class. He was absolutely forthright as he exclaimed that being there was a waste of time for him and that the people who sent him should know that. Still, he couldn't help speaking up in class from time-to-time when the discussion happened to align with his personal views. But for the vast majority of the first 4 or 5 classes, he just sat there, arms crossed looking straight ahead.

Somewhere around that point in time, I visited Bryce's department to work with his team de-briefing the results of their organizational culture survey. The idea was to have them work together as a team and set goals to improve the way they did things as a team. However, this didn't quite happen. The whole discussion seemed thwarted and little was accomplished. Afterward, one of the senior team members pulled me aside and explained that, "Nothing good will come from that discussion. We can never speak our minds without making sure it's in line with what Bryce wants." His control was near absolute. If he liked you and you did everything his way, including saying what he wanted to hear, then all was well. If you crossed him in any way, and this was extremely easy, you could find yourself ostracized, and he always got rid of those he didn't like.

Another part of the development program involved our conducting individual coaching sessions with each of the participants. During these, I consistently challenged Bryce's ways, ideas, paradigms, and the results they had on team culture and performance. The results of these discussions were also reported to Bryce's supervisor.

Bryce's supervisor Karen, took this as an opportunity to try to change things for the better. Frankly, I know that Bryce didn't make it easy for her, to say the least. But she was trying.

Six months later, the program ended, and I found out what we had accomplished with Bryce. As I was leaving the building he pulled up in his car. He put his hand out the window for me to shake and told me that he was impressed. He had been so sure that there was nothing I could teach him, but then he admitted that he had, "Learned a thing or two." For him, this was a huge admission. We talked for about 30-minutes, a conversation that ended with this final glimmer of hope that he really wanted to change; he told me that he would make a real effort to listen better as he saw the benefits for himself and his team.

Checking back six months later, Bryce had been true to his word. His supervisor was still chipping away at his attitude and ways of doing things that are deeply imbedded in Zone 4. Things had improved for his team and everyone else as he was a better listener and somewhat more open to other's ideas.

Key Points of Chapter Five

1. The ZONE 4 Leader's illusionary self-confidence can be so strong that it limits their ability to receive feedback about their performance.

2. The ZONE 4 Leader is likely to have the hardest time understanding their shortcomings and resist making the transition to move toward ZONE 1.

Chapter Six

ZONE Leadership and the Culture Each Creates

ZONE 1	ZONE 2	ZONE 3	ZONE 4
Fully Developed, Fully Conscious	*Not Fully Developed, Fully Conscious*	*Not Fully Developed, Somewhat Conscious*	*Not Developed, Not Conscious*
ZONE 1 – Fully Effective Selfless Genuine Leader	ZONE 2 – Aware of Weaknesses and that Development is Needed	ZONE 3 – Limited Awareness of Actual Weaknesses or Need For Development	ZONE 4 – Unaware of Weaknesses or Need For Development

Over time, organizations tend to take on a predominant culture that mirrors the ZONE makeup of the leaders. Let's look at each of these cultures individually and what it's like to work in them.

Zone 1 Organizational Culture

When the preponderance of leaders are ZONE 1, the culture of the organization is highly effective and it becomes a very desirable place to work.

> *The ZONE 1 culture is a direct reflection of the dominance of the ZONE 1 leaders. As we discuss and use the term "ZONE 1 leader," we are referring to the effect of these leaders and the organizational culture they create.*

Things work well in nearly all areas, and ZONE 1 Leaders tend to have an excellent understanding of one-another's roles and the impact throughout the organization. This allows them to make well-informed decisions based on an accurate consideration of their impact, including second and third order effects.

ZONE 1 Leaders are very clear and direct in their expectations. They remain flexible to changing as necessary around the point of reaching the organization's goals. They are not emotionally tied to any particular idea or course of action; rather they want to do what is most effective. They embrace the concept of being forward-looking through the process of collaboration and barrier-free communication.

ZONE 1 cultures utilize praise and constructive criticism in a balanced approach. Destructive criticism has no place in a ZONE 1 organization, and those who use it are quickly mentored toward understanding its effect and making it constructive instead.

A high degree of loyalty and respect is felt throughout the entire operation. No one needs to take charge of morale, as everyone is part of it and it is quite high. People willingly take more initiative in ZONE 1 organizations as a result of this.

Within a ZONE 1 organization, new hires tend to also be ZONE 1. ZONE 1 hiring managers and committees are drawn to hiring ZONE 1 candidates. They are also adept at identifying ZONE 2, 3, and 4 types and excluding them on that basis. Additionally, ZONE 1 candidates are drawn to ZONE 1 Leaders and organizations and they tend to not accept offers from ZONE 2, 3, or 4 companies. Indeed, ZONE 1 Leaders are the only group having a good handle on assessing leadership skills in others as a separate skill set required for success in leading others.

> *ZONE 1 Leaders and Organizations Primarily Concentrate on Facts*

ZONE 1 Leaders have a great understanding of others, and they use this effectively with leaders who are in ZONEs 2, 3, and 4 to help them develop into better leaders with an eye toward moving them into ZONE 1.

ZONE 1 Leaders do not fire employees without exhausting every option possible to allow others to correct shortfalls and develop, therefore, when someone has to be let go, it is the employee who decided not to develop themselves who really made the choice to leave.

The primary key to becoming and remaining a ZONE 1 Leader is an effective system of mentoring.

ZONE 1 organizations view formal mentoring systems as vital, so for an organization to be at ZONE 1, they must have a formal mentoring system in place at every level of the organization. In a ZONE 1 workplace this just seems natural as everyone is openly expecting great feedback (praise and constructive criticism), coaching, and guidance.

To enhance awareness, ZONE 1 mentoring typically uses formal feedback tools such as 360-degree assessments coupled with validation, and Organizational Culture Surveys. Mentors and mentees actively use these to set specific leadership development goals.

An effective 360-degree feedback survey provides the leader with individualized feedback on their leadership performance from their Supervisor, Peers, Subordinates, and their own Self-assessment.

An effective Organizational Culture Survey provides feedback on the team environment created by the leader, which the leader is responsible and accountable for.

Evaluation and Accountability in ZONE 1 Organizations

Coupled with assessment and feedback, ZONE 1 organizations place emphasis on appropriate responsibility and accountability including proper grading and documentation in their performance evaluation system. In a ZONE 1 culture, ZONE 1 Leaders welcome this. On the other hand, ZONE 2, 3, and 4 Leaders may initially view this as punitive; however this is not the intent of honest and accurate grading in a ZONE 1 culture.

Supervisors and mentors recognize this and work to ensure that ZONE 2, 3, and 4 Leaders view accurate performance evaluation grades and comments as important checks and balances to keep them on track toward development. This is admittedly a fine balancing act to ensure that proper evaluation grades or comments are not perceived as punishment; good or bad, they are earned and it is proper and fair that evaluations reflect this.

Another significant paradigm in ZONE 1 cultures is acceptance of the fact that leaders at all levels are responsible for the leadership performance and development of all subordinate leaders who work for them. The senior leader is accountable for this in their evaluations, and this includes any mismatch between the grades they assign subordinate leaders and the results of those leader's 360-degree feedback surveys, Organizational Culture Surveys, or other evaluating instruments. In other words, if a subordinate leader's evaluation grades don't reflect the feedback their team provides, the senior leader is accountable and this lack of leadership will be included in their performance evaluation.

ZONE 1 Culture Summary

The ZONE 1 culture is marked by selfless openness and honesty at its core. ZONE 1 Leaders are not perfect, but they work to correct issues as they become aware of them and expect the same from all who work for them.

> *The ZONE 1 culture is what we all intrinsically know as the way a workplace ought to be.*

The ZONE 1 culture creates a great workplace that achieves important things with people who are excited by what they do and look forward to coming to work.

Zone 2 Organizational Culture

When the preponderance of leaders are ZONE 2, their collective limitations are magnified producing some level of general inefficiency and inaction.

ZONE 2 organizations are not operating at their potential. Interestingly, this is generally not apparent to those in charge as they tend to accept levels of performance and capacity as they are. However, if senior leaders could see what was possible in a ZONE 1 culture, this change of perspective would make it immediately apparent that working to move all leaders into ZONE 1, and thereby fostering a ZONE 1 culture, is absolutely vital and should be priority #1.

Unfortunately, our observation is that "Self-disabled" ZONE 2 leaders are currently the dominant group throughout the world. This seems to be a reflection of the changes that society has gone through.

We believe that past generations were more selfless. This is evidenced by their expressions of appreciation for even the smallest things and in how they relate to and respect one-another. More recent generations appear to feel more entitled and are therefore more concerned with self than others. This increased emphasis on self is a primary basis behind leaders who are in ZONE 2 long-term.

In the future, it appears that economic factors may motivate a shift back to more selfless attitudes. Because of this, the naturally occurring dominant leadership zone may well change again. Many senior leaders have expressed to us that they are actually waiting for this change to occur. In fact, they are banking on this as the primary way for them to return to a more desirable, ZONE 1 Leadership culture.

> *... if senior leaders could see what was possible in a ZONE 1 culture, this change of perspective would make it immediately apparent that working to move all leaders into ZONE 1, which then creates a ZONE 1 culture, is absolutely vital and should be priority #1.*

The reality is that while they wait, these organizations are operating in ZONE 2, and end up finding themselves stagnant and inept at positioning themselves for the future. They are relying on hope rather than taking the lead. They have become too reactionary rather than strategic and self-starting.

Sadly, we have all seen many organizations in recent years, from smaller ones to large multi-national corporations, fall victim to ZONE 2 attitudes pushing them down the wrong roads, even into bankruptcy and going out of business.

The bottom line again is that, "When the preponderance of leaders are ZONE 2, their collective limitations are magnified producing some level of general inefficiency and inaction."

In ZONE 2 organizations, the collective limitations of the leaders drive the operation. The exact manifestations of this vary depending on the limitations and how they interact, especially the limitations of senior leaders, who have the most influence.

In essence, ZONE 2 Leaders cause many of their own problems. For instance, if the senior leaders shy away from being open, direct, or honest because they view this as confrontational, their model may become the dominant way of doing business and leaders in general may "band-aid" situations instead. This can result in things like poor performance failing to be addressed, improper evaluation marks being assigned, and driving the morale of good performers down in reaction to this unfair and unjust treatment.

> *ZONE 2 Leaders and Organizations Primarily Concentrate on Limitations*

The natural human tendency is to think of self first when another person's self-centered actions affect you negatively, and ZONE 2 behavior can beget ZONE 2 behavior, either directly or as a second or third order effect. So when good performers have a morale drop because they have been wronged, there is no mystery why.

While ZONE 2 Leaders have excellent awareness, their choice in too many cases is to justify their inappropriate actions, or inaction. Again, self comfort and self-preservation come first.

Interestingly, some ZONE 2 Leaders will openly discuss their self-imposed disabilities. When a ZONE 2 Leader says things like, "I know I should talk to Sally about her performance, but she intimidates me," they are modeling what has come to be accepted in many ZONE 2 cultures as acceptable behaviors. If a ZONE 1 Leader were to hear this, they would take action to correct this. But in a ZONE 2 culture, empathy or sympathy with the plight of the ZONE 2 "victim" is the more common response.

When formal mentoring systems are present in ZONE 2 organizations, it is common for the senior leadership to not participate nor make having a mentor a high priority for subordinates. An additional handicap exists in ZONE 2 cultures in that ZONE 2 Leaders cannot effectively mentor others because of their limitations. In fact, it is again not uncommon to find functionally inept or failed mentoring relationships that exist for show, but which produce little value for mentees.

ZONE 2 organizations foster a culture where people outwardly say they want feedback, but it is not used effectively if offered. It is not entirely uncommon for those who offer what is seen as bothersome or controversial feedback to be responded to unfavorably. It is usually made very clear that certain types of feedback are not appreciated and are discouraged. "I'm just going to keep my mouth shut," is an all too common sentiment expressed at many ZONE 2 organizations.

Praise and constructive criticism are not used in a balanced manner thus creating winners and losers which results in much frustration and even personal animosity and grudges. Formal awards are bothersome to many people in ZONE 2 cultures and may work counter to what was intended in some cases, especially if those who are perceived as undeserving receive awards.

Evaluation and Accountability in ZONE 2 Organizations

ZONE 2 organizations tend to place uneven emphasis on appropriate responsibility and accountability. Honest and accurate grading in the evaluation system is likely to be looked at with negativity, as in how it will affect "me" if events such as layoffs occur. Grading tends to be inflated, and comments lacking in documenting actual performance. It is therefore more difficult or impossible to use evaluations to validate performance or provide accountability. Actual superior performers often feel that their evaluations are cheapened because of these inconsistencies and grade inflation.

Supervisors tend to give good marks without supporting comments in an effort to avoid accountability for themselves. Some ZONE 2 Leaders will also dump their responsibility on subordinates, directing them to self-evaluate and write their own evaluations. Finally, in many ZONE 2 cultures, evaluations are submitted so late as to communicate to subordinates that the leadership places almost no importance on doing this for their people, and that the jobs they do have little significance.

ZONE 2 cultures rarely hold senior leaders properly accountable for the effectiveness of subordinate leaders under them, nor is this included in either the grading or comments in the senior leader's evaluations.

ZONE 2 Culture Summary

The ZONE 2 culture is marked by limitations, mostly self-imposed. ZONE 2 Leaders tend to be overly concerned with self in the areas that they are ineffective. This creates a fragmented workplace that usually achieves its basic purpose, but does not operate at true capacity.

Morale is haphazard and there are many opportunities for de-motivation. ZONE 2 cultures usually leave those who work there with the feeling of uncertainty and wanting things to change for the better.

ZONE 2 cultures have become quite common and have added to workers seeing their jobs as insecure environments, therefore always having their resume out there and being ready to move on if required.

Zone 3 Organizational Culture

Sometimes, though rarely, an organization can exist with a preponderance of the leaders being ZONE 3 types. However the information flow is so poor that they might blindly "walk off a cliff" together and wonder how it happened.

We have come across a limited number of ZONE 3 businesses, usually made up of only a single person. These businesses exist in spite of this ZONE 3 owner/worker because the product or service provided is highly sought after or indispensible, and there is limited or no competition. Customers don't like doing business with them, but they either have no choice or are willing to put up with the ZONE 3 person because the product is so good. Again, they exist in spite of themselves.

A more common ZONE 3 occurrence is for the people working under the ZONE 3 Leader to take up the slack and make things run as they should. The interactions the team has with the ZONE 3 leader are few and amount to mostly lip-service. The ZONE 3 leader has no real affect on the culture, which is actually defined by those taking up the slack. The culture created in these instances is typically ZONE 2. So we end up with a ZONE 2 culture being lead (on paper at least) by a ZONE 3 Leader who has been minimized or excluded.

But by-far, the most common way for a ZONE 3 culture to be formed is as the result of the collective limitations of a group of ZONE 2 Leaders. Limitations on the effective sharing of information is the key factor that makes up this ZONE 3 culture and the ZONE 2 Leaders involved will do this for a variety of reasons.

As an example, a "Self-disabled" ZONE 2 Leader may fail to share information he or she thinks is controversial or risky for fear of being held accountable. On the other hand, an "Out-for-#1" ZONE 2 Leader who sees information as power may fail to share the same information in an attempt to retain this perceived power. These are only two reasons that ZONE 2 Leaders might not share information freely; there are as many actual reasons as there are ZONE 2 Leader limitations.

> *When ZONE 2 limitations collectively cause a ZONE 3 culture, over-concern with self is at the heart of the problem.*

Another common example of a ZONE 2 Leader creating a ZONE 3 culture is when the leader clearly states what they don't want to hear and shuts down certain inputs. We are not talking about the leader steering an off-track discussion back on track, rather, this is when the leader flat out tells others what they don't want. Others, except ZONE 1, will readily follow this direction, especially if done in a "not-so-nice" tone.

We have observed these ZONE 2 information issues and ZONE 3 "mini-cultures" most often in meetings and conferences. The higher up the senior attendees or participants, the more thwarted the information flow seems to be.

Conversations in the hall during breaks or after the meeting reveal the ZONE 3 nature of the group. You may hear an individual saying something like, "What a waste of time and money! The boss is way off on this thing and everyone in there knows it except her. Someone should really say something, but they're all too busy kissing up instead. I would love to, but then I'd probably be branded as insubordinate for disagreeing with them all and I'm not about to get my head chopped off."

Unfortunately this is something we've probably all experienced, and graphically illustrates the key issue in a ZONE 3 culture – ineffectiveness and inefficiency caused by poor communication flow.

Zone 4 Organizational Culture

In a ZONE 4 culture, the leader is the sole determinant of the culture. No others have any significant input. The ZONE 4 Leader strongly believes and projects that their way is the right way. As long as everyone else defers to this and goes along, there is harmony. Creative thought is extremely limited and restricted to the leader's viewpoint, and information flow is restricted.

For example, if a subordinate has a difference of opinion or tries to point out anything the leader or group could do differently, they may be viewed by the ZONE 4 Leader as a threat. The result is that the leader will immediately, and forcefully, try to get this person in line with their perspective. There is no "agree-to-disagree" here. If the subordinate refuses, the ZONE 4 Leader is likely to declare them ostracized and seek to get rid of them as soon as possible.

When dealing with higher-ups, the ZONE 4 Leader will likely just ignore feedback or different points of view because of their strong belief that they are right, unless forced.

The bottom line in ZONE 4 cultures is that as long as the ZONE 4 Leader is kept happy, all appears well.

Key Points of Chapter Six

1. The primary determinant of workplace culture is, in most cases, the ZONE in which the preponderance of leaders are developed to.

2. The way to change the culture is to develop the leaders. They will then naturally change the culture to match their Leadership ZONE.

3. When the difference between a ZONE 1 culture and other ZONE cultures are examined, it becomes clear that all organizations should be working toward developing ZONE 1 Leaders as a primary initiative.

4. ZONE 1 Leaders and Organizations Primarily Concentrate on Facts.

5. ZONE 2 Leaders and Organizations Primarily Concentrate on Limitations.

6. The ZONE 1 culture is what we all intrinsically know as the way a workplace ought to be.

Chapter Seven

How to Move to a ZONE 1 Culture

ZONE 1	ZONE 2	ZONE 3	ZONE 4
Fully Developed, Fully Conscious	*Not Fully Developed, Fully Conscious*	*Not Fully Developed, Somewhat Conscious*	*Not Developed, Not Conscious*
ZONE 1 – Fully Effective Selfless Genuine Leader	ZONE 2 – Aware of Weaknesses and that Development is Needed	ZONE 3 – Limited Awareness of Actual Weaknesses or Need For Development	ZONE 4 – Unaware of Weaknesses or Need For Development

Developing a ZONE 1 culture is a two step process. First work to develop individuals as ZONE 1 Leaders. Second, these ZONE 1 Leaders will then work to develop their team into a ZONE 1 culture.

While it is the ideal that this shift to ZONE 1 be a fully supported effort that starts with the top leader, there are many circumstances where this may not be the case. The good news is that any individual leader can decide and take action to become ZONE 1, and also create a ZONE 1 culture with those below them.

In fact, this could be the way to move the larger culture toward ZONE 1 – when others see the results; this may be the spark they need. This is true ZONE 1 Leadership – leading effectively from whatever position a person may hold.

Like many worthwhile initiatives, the basic steps are straightforward. We'll first look at the ZONE 1 Leader development process, and then discuss how to work to create a ZONE 1 culture.

The ZONE 1 Leader Development Process

1. Seek to understand who you are as a leader; your personality and comfort zones.
2. Get feedback from others on your leadership performance; identify weaknesses.
3. Work with your mentor to develop goals and action plans.
4. Take action, evaluate progress and results.
5. Repeat this process for continuous improvement.

Seek To Understand Who You Are As A Leader; Your Personality and Comfort Zones. To know more about whom you are at your core and how you relate to the world, it is useful to obtain informal observations from those who know you well, or utilize formal self-assessment instruments.

Your areas of comfort usually relate to your areas of leadership effectiveness, while your areas of discomfort usually relate to your areas of leadership weakness. It is useful to spend time analyzing these areas to help in the identification of things you need to work on to attain ZONE 1.

In respect to formal assessment instruments, the authors of ZONE 1 Leadership utilize the Myers-Briggs Type Indicator© and the ZONE 1 Leadership Styles Inventory© in their consulting practice. The combination of these instruments relates who a person is to the leadership styles they choose. This relation has direct correlation to one's areas of comfort and discomfort.

Get Feedback From Others On Your Leadership Performance; Identify Weaknesses. Talk to your supervisor, peers, and trusted senior subordinates to get feedback on your leadership performance and the results it has on the team. You are looking for specific things you are doing and if they are being interpreted as intended. You should also gain a heightened awareness of your blind areas that result in unknowingly negative results with your team. The overall goal is finding out what others see as important for you to correct within yourself to attain ZONE 1.

In respect to formal assessment instruments, the authors of ZONE 1 Leadership utilize the ZONE 1 Leadership 360-Degree Feedback Survey$^©$ and ZONE 1 Leadership Results Culture Survey$^©$ in their consulting practice. The combination of these instruments provides the leader with feedback from their team on their leadership performance and the culture created as a result.

Work With Your Mentor To Develop Goals And Action Plans. Establish a mentoring relationship with a known ZONE 1 Leader. Define your current level of commitment to developing into a ZONE 1 Leader, and what your development is going to entail from this point forward.

Prioritize specific weaknesses and shortfalls that you need to correct.

Set a minimum of one, but no more than three development goals. This will allow you to focus on what will have the most meaning, significance, and will produce the most substantial results. (Please see Appendix A for a discussion of effective development goals).

> *Make your goals significant. No busy work here!*

Take Action, Evaluate Progress And Results. Act with purpose and tenacity. ZONE 1 development goals should be at the forefront of the way you think and act throughout your day.

Evaluate your progress continuously. Concentrate on outcomes; what are the impacts and results of your actions? Include second and third order outcomes in your awareness.

Seek accurate feedback from a balance of people. This feedback needs to come from those who will give you their honest and open critical observations. It is vital for you to understand how your natural reactions, expressions of emotion, ways of saying things, etc. affect others.

Confer with your mentor as soon as possible to discuss what you find out. Make adjustments based on your needs for growth in relation to the needs of your team and the organization as a whole. This is useful in identifying and addressing actions you find uncomfortable or difficult.

Always be open to revising your goals to ensure they remain significant. Don't be afraid to drop a goal and add a new goal.

Repeat This Process For Continuous Improvement. Repeat! Repeat! Repeat!

ZONE 1 Leaders realize they will need a mentor(s) throughout their leadership life and are continuously challenging themselves for ways to enhance their performance as leaders throughout this journey.

Now let's look at how to utilize ZONE 1 Leadership in developing a ZONE 1 Organizational Culture.

The ZONE 1 Organizational Culture Development Process

1. Establish a ZONE 1 Leader Development Initiative.
2. Get feedback from all employees on organizational culture.
3. Develop team goals and action plans.
4. Take action, evaluate progress and results.
5. Repeat this process for continuous improvement.

Establish a ZONE 1 Leader Development Initiative. There are three significant elements to a ZONE 1 initiative.

First is a ZONE 1 Leadership Mentoring System. This is the key to effective ZONE 1 development, therefore all leaders, including the top leader, must have a formal mentor. Ideally, these mentors should be ZONE 1 leaders. While this is the ideal, it may not be initially possible to achieve this, in which case the mentors chosen need to be as close to ZONE 1 as possible, and should operate under the tutelage of a ZONE 1 Leader.

Second is Accountability. This starts with an open and honest atmosphere. Supervisors and mentors should be privy to everything pertaining to the ZONE 1 developing leaders they are working with. This includes all feedback assessments. Additionally, the evaluation system, organization-wide, must be uniform, fair, and honest. This allows it to act as an effective validation and accountability tool.

<u>Third, support from the highest levels is vital.</u> The top leader and all senior executive staff must be on the same page and take ZONE 1 development seriously. They must convey that this is not just another "fad" program that will come and go, but that it will end up changing all the leaders and the team into being selfless, fully effective, and genuine. It will not take long for the idea that this might be a "fad" to vanish, but that can only happen if there is proper support and involvement by the entire senior leadership team. In other words, all senior leaders must act in a ZONE 1 manner immediately in order for the initiative to succeed.

Get Feedback From All Employees On Organizational Culture. ZONE 1 Leaders and ZONE 1 cultures operate on facts.

A specific type of Organizational Culture survey must be conducted and repeated regularly in order for every employee to know where things stand and work as a team to develop the culture toward ZONE 1.

This survey must be designed to gather feedback from every employee about how their team is functioning in relation to a ZONE 1 culture. It should be relatively short and stay on point. It should not include opinion polls, questions about the physical environment, or any other items that do not directly assess how the team is functioning. Repeating the exact same survey at regular intervals, such as annually, provides benchmarks and trend analysis which are vital facts to ZONE 1 cultures.

In respect to the culture survey, the authors of ZONE 1 Leadership™ utilize the ZONE 1 Leadership Results Culture Survey© in their consulting practice. This instrument provides feedback from all employees on the team culture created as a result of the leadership.

Develop Team Goals And Action Plans. In a ZONE 1 culture, the results of the organizational culture survey are shared with all employees, but in a very specific way. First, the executive staff will review the culture survey and pick out any items they will take for action. They will detail their goals and plans in writing.

Individual leaders, guided by their ZONE 1 mentor, will then discuss their specific team results with the entire team and work together to reach consensus and set specific goals and action plans to move the team culture toward ZONE 1. They will also brief the team on items the executive staff has taken for action and review their written goals and plans. These discussions need to happen in as timely a manner as possible following completion of the survey in order to enhance their relevance.

Using the culture survey results in this way, instead of restricting who gets to see the results, will have an immediate and lasting effect on the culture. It specifically works to build esprit-de-corps, or morale, and ownership by every employee in the development of ZONE 1 plans and actions. It also works to provide maximum accountability at every level resulting in the culture being the best for all employees. The time investment is minimal considering the potential outcome.

Take Action, Evaluate Progress And Results. The team and those assigned to lead specific ZONE 1 team development goals should evaluate progress continuously. They should concentrate on outcomes; what are the impact and results of actions? They should seek accurate feedback from everyone affected to ensure honest and open critical observations.

The teams should discuss progress as part of their regular team meetings and make adjustments to their actions as they go to remain on track toward goal attainment. They should also be open to revising team goals and plans to ensure they remain significant.

One benefit that underlies these team efforts is that it frees the leader in terms of both time and focus because the team becomes increasingly self-directed. This allows the leader to then become more forward-looking and strategic in their focus. In fact, at some point, the leadership will likely need to strategically rethink the entire direction and way the organization does business because the evolving ZONE 1 culture will result in a whole new set of organizational capacities and capabilities.

Leading a mature and focused ZONE 1 team vs. a limited ZONE 2, 3, or 4 team opens up many new possibilities and opportunities, and quite frankly, is fun to lead.

Repeat This Process For Continuous Improvement. Repeat! Repeat! Repeat!

ZONE 1 organizations must be diligent at maintaining themselves in ZONE 1.

Those who are part of the efforts to get to ZONE 1 understand how they did it. As new people are added and older ones leave, the understanding of this experience within the team begins to fade. New people bring their ways with them, some of which are undesirable. If not actively maintained, even the most solidly built ZONE 1 culture can erode as people adopt or revert to undesirable ways.

ZONE 1 cultures must therefore continuously challenge themselves for ways to enhance their organizations and remain in ZONE 1 throughout their journey together.

The Role of Formal Assessment Tools in Developing ZONE 1 Leaders and Moving to a ZONE 1 Culture

A leader cannot understand the true impact of his or her actions by merely looking at the apparent outcome. One must also be able to know and understand the thoughts and feelings of those affected by the leader's actions to understand the true impact with any degree of accuracy.

We cannot know or deduce these things independently ourselves.

The primary role of well designed formal assessments is to reveal this inner knowledge so that we can relate outcomes to what is intended, and track trends.

Key Points of Chapter Seven

1. Developing a ZONE 1 culture is a two step process. First work to develop individuals as ZONE 1 Leaders. They will then work to develop those under them into the ZONE 1 culture.

2. There are three significant elements to a ZONE 1 initiative:
    a. ZONE 1 Leadership Mentoring System.
    b. Accountability System.
    c. Integrated System, support from highest level is vital.

3. ZONE 1 Leaders realize they will need a mentor(s) throughout their leadership life and are continuously challenging themselves for ways to enhance themselves throughout this journey.

4. A specific type of Organizational Culture survey must be conducted and repeated regularly in order for every employee to know where things stand and work as a team to develop the culture toward ZONE 1.

5. ZONE 1 organizations must be diligent at maintaining themselves in ZONE 1.

Appendix A

How to Set Effective Development Goals

The Zone 1 Development Goal Process is different from what you may have experienced in the past.

First of all, only set goals of true significance and your motivation will naturally follow. Revise, add, delete, or otherwise modify your goals to keep them significant. Goals that lack significance tend to be easily set aside. If your goals don't intrinsically motivate you, they are probably too small or insignificant, and you should get bigger and better goals.

Second, set no more than three goals at a time. If these are of true significance, you will make large strides very quickly. Too many small goals tend to distract or water down action.

Most of the methods and models we've come across for goal setting concentrate on the goal statement and what should go into it. These typically include such things as being sure the goal is specific, measureable, time-phased, etc.

We have found that more time spent in fleshing things out after the goal is properly stated is vital to success. After all, it only takes a few minutes to state the goal, but may take many weeks, months, and even years to achieve it.

Some goals, especially leadership development goals, may not have a firm deadline.

For instance, many leaders recognize that they need to develop better listening skills and habits. If you set a goal to listen better, what would the deadline be? Such "open-ended" goals are vital to achieve ZONE 1 Leadership effectiveness.

There are four specific areas in the Zone 1 Development Goal Model. We will use a sample goal of "Overcoming Fear of Confrontation" as an illustration to discuss each of these:

❶ State the goal

This is a straightforward statement of what you want to achieve. For example:

> *Overcome my fear of confronting others*

❷ **What's been accomplished so far and what still needs to be accomplished to achieve the goal?**

Think specifically about where things stand and where you need to go. This should include your thoughts about weaknesses and shortfalls that need to be overcome. For example:

> *I am very uncomfortable speaking to certain people on my team about their performance. They intimidate me.*
>
> *My action thus far is to avoid discussing things with others that might lead to confrontation, such as trying to correct a subordinate's unacceptable performance. I've been this way for my entire life, but it has really become an issue during my last 16 years in different leadership positions.*
>
> *I am also very apprehensive about giving less than perfect marks or negative comments on performance evaluations.*
>
> *This has turned into a serious problem for me. I know I am not acting in the way I should as a leader, yet I feel powerless when this fear grips me. I have come to hate this part of me and my self-esteem gets lower every time I avoid doing what I know I should be doing.*

❸ **Action plan**

This includes setting deadlines, detailing any resources or support you may need, and a schedule to review your actions with your ZONE 1 Mentor or others as appropriate for accountability. This helps to ensure your goal remains significant and you remain motivated. For example:

> *Research available books, DVD's, and possible courses of instruction that might exist to help to develop my knowledge and abilities (Deadline: July 28).*
>
> *Stop avoiding situations that I fear might lead to confrontation. Ask my ZONE 1 Mentor and Supervisor, who are both skilled at assertion, to help me develop an action plan to overcome my fears (Deadline: August 7).*
>
> *Ask both my ZONE 1 Mentor and Supervisor to coach me, role play with me, and honestly help me to develop some level of comfort (Deadline: Ongoing).*
>
> *Review my actions and progress with my Zone 1 Mentor during our regular weekly meeting (Deadline: Ongoing), and with my Supervisor as events occur (Deadline: Ongoing).*

❹ Indications of Success

Define both formal and informal measures of performance. What you should be looking for to know you are moving in the right direction and accomplishing what you want to achieve. For example:

Self-evaluation: Develop actual confidence speaking with others about their performance and in other situations where confrontation occurs.

Successful encounters with subordinates when talking about their performance instead of my avoiding or backing down too easily- being treated with respect by others.

Positive feedback from my ZONE 1 Mentor and Supervisor based on actual successful encounters.

Positive feedback from my annual 360-Degree Survey and Organizational Culture Survey.

In summary, remember that only goals of true significance will intrinsically motivate you. This underlying fact is the basic key to successfully developing into a ZONE 1 Leader.

Blank ZONE 1 development goal forms are available for free download at "zone1leadership.com"

Appendix B

The Role Our Values Play In ZONE 1 Development

The framework to every person's actions is based upon their value system. These values come from cultural experiences, family, and every moment that a person has lived and experienced, as if a video camera was recording from birth to the current moment. These values are the decision-making points that define our character. They are unique in the power that they have in how we make decisions. They are also unique in that no other individual can have the same exact value system, as no one else could have had exactly the same experiences. These values operate at a subconscious level, so it's common that people don't understand why they are making the decisions they make, except that it just feels normal.

Think of the moments that you had when interacting with others and coming to an agreement on something, only to find out later that they did something different than what you thought. It may not be the case of not keeping the agreement, but that their value system (how they process information/situations) may have simply been skewed (from your perspective) by their beliefs, their past history, and how they end up generalizing and distorting the information discussed during the agreement with you.

By understanding one's own value system, sound decisions based on fact can be made, while controlling emotional impulses that are formulated from our perceptions and assumptions (that all others should follow based on our value system). In society today this inability to separate fact from assumptions is obvious, and leads to many problems.

We are not suggesting that if we understand our own and others values that we're going to be able to communicate in a manner that always has a feeling of agreement. We are suggesting that conflicts and disagreements can be understood and responded to more effectively by being open to the concepts that: ❶ People make decisions and conclusions (their values) based on past experiences, ❷ You can't change others values, you can only influence them by understanding yours and responding to theirs respectfully, and ❸ Your values change by exposure to new concepts and perspectives that affect your personal interests, so understanding the reasoning of what you do or want is critical.

ZONE 1 Leaders are aware of this and in every situation utilize these perspectives in getting the best out of themselves and others.

In the case of Zone 2, 3 and 4 Leaders, it's important to remember that their values seem natural to them. Their values pull on them like gravity to do what they find comfortable instead of what is most effective as they struggle to develop toward selfless genuine leadership.

Helping ZONE 2, 3, and 4 Leaders recognize the limitations their values are placing on them is a significant foundational step in influencing them to decide to change and embrace their opportunities for growth in becoming a ZONE 1 Leader themselves.

Appendix C

The Three Essential Skills of Open and Honest Communication

As a ZONE 1 Leader, you need to have certain core skills to allow open and honest communication. Those skills consist of patient listening, how to be a properly assertive leader, and concern and understanding of the real needs of others.

Zone 2, 3, and 4 Leaders usually require development in some or all of these skills to allow them to move toward becoming a ZONE 1 Leader.

Patient Listening
When I was young, ambitious and motivated, I remember having what I thought was a "brilliant" idea about how to do something better. I don't remember what the idea was, but I do remember that when I tried to share my great insight with my supervisor, I was cut off in the middle of a sentence and told that my idea wouldn't work. "We've done that before," or "We've tried that

before and it didn't work," I don't remember the exact words my supervisor used, but the message was clear.

I do remember feeling hurt and frustrated because I didn't get listened to. I remember walking away saying something like, "Why didn't he listen to me? He didn't even let me get my point across. What's wrong with him?" I left that encounter a little less motivated, and a little gun-shy toward suggesting anything in the future.

Has that ever happened to you as a subordinate? Have you ever failed to listen to another as a leader?

Listening is a discipline that many leaders do not practice effectively. I would go so far as to say that in my experience, listening is the most ill practiced leadership skill, yet we all know that we need to listen effectively to lead effectively.

With listening comes another word: Patience

My mother used to tell me that, "Patience is a virtue." Maybe your mother said the same thing to you. Why would my mother consider patience to be a virtue? Possibly because so many people fail to exercise patience – and they frequently show it in their poor listening skills!

Patient listening doesn't just automatically happen. It requires conscious thought.

The truth is that we all have to exercise our conscious intent to be patient because listening and patience are active, not automatic actions. We can't condition or train ourselves to do these two properly without consciously thinking about them as we do them.

Honor others by "Being There"

So the next time someone is communicating to you, do that other person the honor of giving your full attention. Listen intently with the goal of hearing and really understanding what that person is saying – not half-listening or listening with the intent of responding (getting your two-cents in).

Stay conscious and be known as a leader who patiently listens and understands. You'll have a better team and you'll make better decisions, because; "Wisdom is not a product of thought. The deep knowing that is wisdom arises through the simple act of giving someone or something your full attention." - Eckhart Tolle

How To Be A Properly Assertive Leader
Many leaders struggle with being assertive in the right way and at the right time. Consider this story:

> *My name is Tony and I run the customer service section at our local branch office. Last month our operations were being reviewed by a corporate team led by the Regional Office Manager. While he and I were going over our ISO-*

9001 processes, we were distracted by Sylvia, a senior member of my team, who was talking loudly with another worker. I personally find it difficult to deal with Sylvia. She intimidates me so I mostly try to stick to small talk and avoid crossing her.

The Regional Manager was annoyed with her loud voice. I prayed she would stop! When she didn't, he prodded me with a look to, "Go take care of that!"

With a lump in my throat, I approached and tried to quietly shush Sylvia. She looked at me with scorn and whispered, "Oh am I being too loud?" then went back to her conversation with a nasty glance back at me. I tried again and she ignored me. I'd had enough and thoughtlessly yelled "Shut up!" which is what the Regional Manager saw and heard as he walked up behind me.

He immediately took me into my office and had a formal counseling session with me about being disrespectful and too coercive, and directed me to apologize to Sylvia. How ironic and frustrating! I'm on the pad for being too hard, when I'm actually too passive! My future is in the toilet and I'm thinking of just quitting.

As with Tony, others will not respect and follow a leader who is too passive and lets others walk all over them. Being too passive can also lead to being indecisive, taking on work one shouldn't, or withholding vital information especially if it is bad news or unpopular. Too passive usually equals wimpy.

On the other hand, being too assertive is also hard for others to respect as it may leave them feeling pushed around, not listened to, manipulated, or dominated. Excessive assertiveness can also result in micro-management. Too assertive usually equals pushy, or even aggressive.

Interestingly, being too passive or too assertive both come from the same place in us as we unconsciously concentrate on the wrong thing - how we personally feel. Specifically we are operating from our comfort zone rather than thinking about and doing what is right for the team of people working for us. In both cases, the team knows this and loses respect and esprit-de-corps.

If this is you – too pushy or too passive – there are several things you can do to help apply these vital skills with the balance necessary to lead effectively.

> First, consciously refocus yourself on doing what is right for your team instead of what makes you personally feel comfortable or avoiding discomfort.
>
> Second, get a good mentor. Nothing is more effective at helping you deal with your shortfalls. Dissect past occurrences that went wrong, and then practice with your mentor the right way to think, act, and communicate. Also strategize with your mentor as new situations arise to fully retrain yourself and gain confidence with these skills.
>
> Third, remain diligent at consciously focusing on doing what is right for your team instead of your personal

comfort. There is strength for you in this higher purpose. Your team will respect that you've changed, after a time, and will come to know that you are out for them rather than yourself. This is leadership others can willingly support and follow.

Concern for and Understanding The Real Needs Of Others
It's easy to misunderstand another person if all we know is what they say, do, or think, without understanding why.

What we say, do, or think = Our **Position**.

Why we say, do, or think something = Our **Interest**.

Unfortunately, our world operates in a position-based framework. All of us are experts at saying what we think, but novices in many respects at revealing what drives us to think that way. The same holds true for what we say, and what we do.

Likewise, we are experts at observing others on the surface, but rarely seek to understand why they are that way.

Because we are operating within this "positional thinking," we find it easy to criticize, condemn, and complain about others. This is the way of the world and completely accepted (within certain boundaries).

The result is evident in the over-abundance of ZONE 2, 3 and 4 Leaders in our society today.

ZONE 1 Leaders have a clear understanding of the positions of others, but they also focus on understanding the underlying interests that drive others decisions.

ZONE 1 Leaders avoid getting caught up in conflicts caused by "positional opposition." Their understanding of others interests allows them to be selfless and bring the team to a place of constructive dialog.

In summary, to be a ZONE 1 Leader, one must take the time to:

1. Patiently listen to what others have to say.

2. Express with appropriate assertiveness an open and honest insight of the obvious and less obvious behaviors of others.

3. Work in an increasingly selfless manner to understand and utilize both positions and interests for the good of others and the team.

Appendix D

A Message for ZONE 2, 3, and 4 Leaders on Mentoring

Throughout this book we discuss and emphasize the importance of a formal ZONE 1 mentor. Formal mentors are an instrumental piece to becoming and nurturing yourself as a ZONE 1 Leader. Without a mentor, it is hard to become and maintain performance as a selfless genuine leader.

Beyond the formal role of mentoring, informal mentoring occurs continuously. Many would also suggest that our informal mentors have an impact at least as important to us as our personal values in determining who we are and how we respond to situations.

Furthermore, our informal mentors may have influenced us in either a positive or negative way, thus giving us insights into behaviors that we choose to use, or consciously decide <u>not</u> to replicate.

I remember a supervisor that I had while serving in the military. Sam loved the military and what it stood for, though he hadn't been formally trained in how to lead people, only how to manage them. The approach he used with his employees was interpreted by many as rude, insulting, demeaning, and many felt it delivered unproductive results. Sam if asked, would probably not realize that he was "informally mentoring" his team.

I'm sure many of us have had Sam's in our lives at one point, and our natural impulse is to compare them to other people whose mentoring standards fit us better.

The surprising thing about informal mentoring is that the majority of the time, we don't even realize that we are doing it. This could be with staff, family members, anyone you interact with.

I can't count the times when my 6-year old said something or responded to a situation off-the-cuff, and wondered where she learned that. I realize that most of that burden falls on me as it is most likely a manifestation of my "informal mentoring."

Remember, that whatever you do or say, someone is watching, listening, and learning.

If you are a ZONE 2, 3, or 4 Leader, others are learning from what you do and will ultimately model your behavior. If that behavior involves doing what you know you should <u>not</u>, or failing to do what you know you should, the effect on others is completely predictable.

Simply put, if your team or organizational culture is poor, you don't have far to go to find the cause, or more importantly the person that can act to improve the culture, just look in the mirror.

ZONE 1 Leaders take responsibility for the culture of their team and work to nurture and care for it.

Appendix E

A Collection of Key Points

ZONE 1	ZONE 2	ZONE 3	ZONE 4
Fully Developed, Fully Conscious	*Not Fully Developed, Fully Conscious*	*Not Fully Developed, Somewhat Conscious*	*Not Developed, Not Conscious*
ZONE 1 – Fully Effective Selfless Genuine Leader	ZONE 2 – Aware of Weaknesses and that Development is Needed	ZONE 3 – Limited Awareness of Actual Weaknesses or Need For Development	ZONE 4 – Unaware of Weaknesses or Need For Development

Chapter One – Overview of ZONE Leadership:

1. Leadership skills are different from other job skills and must be acknowledged as a unique skill-set.

2. Leaders may settle into zones of comfort, or zones that avoid discomfort. While either of these may seem personally correct, they can be destructive if they are not also right for the team.

3. ZONE 1 Leaders are fully effective selfless genuine leaders. ZONE 1 Leadership skills can be developed as we come across our limitations and use them to our advantage.

Chapter Two – ZONE 1 Leaders:

1. Both natural and developed leaders operate in ZONE 1 as Fully Effective Selfless Genuine Leaders.

2. ZONE 1 Leaders make fewer and fewer mistakes as they continually develop. They strive to make each mistake only once, correct it, and then grow from it.

3. ZONE 1 Leaders have the ability to read and react to what is right for the team as things develop. They are not stuck in any pre-conceived box.

4. In order to be a fully effective ZONE 1 Leader, you must also be a fully effective manager.

5. Selfless service is the hallmark of being a genuine leader. To do anything less is simply not acceptable.

Chapter Three – ZONE 2 Leaders:

1. ZONE 2 leaders are fully conscious and aware of their weaknesses which can be a significant advantage if they use this awareness effectively.

2. ZONE 2 leaders may want to see themselves as being ZONE 1 except for having some shortfalls. This is not valid because part time effectiveness is simply not the same as being a "Fully Effective Selfless Genuine Leader"

3. Every time you see a failing leader that is not being helped effectively, you are actually seeing at least two failing leaders, because it is the higher-up leader's responsibility to make sure their subordinate leaders are effective.

Chapter Four – ZONE 3 Leaders:

1. Care needs to be taken when choosing who to put in charge, whether in an interim situation or as part of the regular selection process.

2. Leaders who are ineffective can develop themselves into ZONE 1, with proper assistance.

3. ZONE 1 Leaders are able to be fully effective mentors. Mentors who are not in ZONE 1 themselves will not be fully effective mentors.

Chapter Five – ZONE 4 Leaders:

1. The ZONE 4 Leader's illusionary self-confidence can be so strong that it limits their ability to receive feedback about their performance.

2. The ZONE 4 Leader is likely to have the hardest time understanding their shortcomings and resist making the transition to move toward ZONE 1.

Chapter Six – ZONE Leadership And The Culture Each Creates:

1. The primary determinant of workplace culture is, in most cases, the ZONE in which the preponderance of leaders are developed to.

2. The way to change the culture is to develop the leaders. They will then naturally change the culture to match their Leadership ZONE.

3. When the difference between a ZONE 1 culture and other ZONE cultures are examined, it becomes clear that all organizations should be working toward developing ZONE 1 Leaders as a primary initiative.

4. ZONE 1 Leaders and Organizations Primarily Concentrate on Facts.

5. ZONE 2 Leaders and Organizations Primarily Concentrate on Limitations.

6. The ZONE 1 culture is what we all intrinsically know as the way a workplace ought to be.

Chapter Seven – How To Move To A ZONE 1 Culture:

1. Developing a ZONE 1 culture is a two step process. First work to develop individuals as ZONE 1 Leaders. They will then work to develop those under them into the ZONE 1 culture.

2. There are three significant elements to a ZONE 1 initiative:
    a. ZONE 1 Leadership Mentoring System.
    b. Accountability System.
    c. Integrated System, support from highest level is vital.

3. ZONE 1 Leaders realize they will need a mentor(s) throughout their leadership life and are continuously challenging themselves for ways to enhance themselves throughout this journey.

4. A specific type of Organizational Culture survey must be conducted and repeated regularly in order for every employee to know where things stand and work as a team to develop the culture toward ZONE 1.

5. ZONE 1 organizations must be diligent at maintaining themselves in ZONE 1.

Acknowledgements

This book has benefited from the ideas, critiques, reviews, or other contributions by many friends, colleagues, and professional acquaintances. We are sincerely grateful for the time and talent each of these wonderful people contributed to help make ZONE 1 Leadership a reality. Thank you all!

Mr. Michael Conklin
Ms. Karen Byron
Ms. Denise Di Giovanni Wessels
Ms. Charlotte Evans
Ms. Tammy Evans
Ms. Patricia Harrington
COL F. William Smullen (U.S. Army Ret)
Mr. Howard Swain
Ms. Susan Virgil
Ms. Lindsay Walsh

Made in the USA
Charleston, SC
13 January 2013